G

The Essence of Living

by
Jerry Savelle

HARRISON HOUSE
Tulsa, Oklahoma

Unless otherwise indicated,
all Scripture quotations are taken from
the *King James Version* of the Bible.

2nd Printing
Over 20,000 in Print

GIVING: The Essence of Living
ISBN 0-89274-250-X
Copyright © 1982 by Jerry Savelle
P. O. Box 2228
Fort Worth, Texas 76113

Published by Harrison House, Inc.
P. O. Box 35035
Tulsa, Oklahoma 74135

Contents

Introduction

In October of 1981 while ministering with Brother Kenneth Copeland in the East Coast Believers Convention in Charlotte, North Carolina, I received a supernatural visitation of the Lord in my hotel room.

In this visit He shared some very important principles with me. The essence of what He told me was that His people are in financial bondage. He told me, ''I want My people out of this bondage. I'm going to divinely intervene on their behalf over the next few years, and I'm going to deliver them, if they will do what I say.'' Then He revealed to me the keys to financial deliverance.

In these pages I am going to share these keys with you. They are not something which I conceived, nor something I had searched for on my own. The Lord outlined them to me supernaturally.

He told me, ''I'm giving you the assignment to go tell My people what I have told you.''

As a result of this assignment, I had to resign the church of which I was founder and pastor, and to merge it with another congregation, so that I could have the freedom to travel and busy myself as I've never done before. This assignment also demanded national television coverage. My schedule immediately became heavier.

It is absolutely essential that I get this message to the Body of Christ: **Jesus of Nazareth is going to set us free and put us in the place we should be financially, so we can get the Gospel**

out and reach multitudes with it before His return.

God wants you to be financially free. Dwell on that. Meditate on it. Keep repeating it; and don't let the Devil talk you out of it.

You may be thinking, "But I don't know if that means me or not." Well, let me assure you, if you are a member of the Body of Christ, that is precisely who this refers to — *you!* You are the very one Jesus gave me this message for!

Do you remember the account of Jesus' going back to His hometown of Nazareth where He went into the temple and stood up to read the Scriptures? Luke tells us:

And there was delivered unto him the book of the prophet Esaias. And when he had opened the book, he found the place where it was written,

*The Spirit of the Lord is upon me, because **he hath anointed me to preach*** *the gospel to the poor* . . . .

Luke 4:17,18

The book of Hebrews tells us that in times past God spoke to us by the prophets, but in these days (and we're in the last days!) He has spoken unto us by His Son. (Heb. 1:1,2.) Well, I can't find a single scripture anywhere which says that Jesus has quit speaking. Jesus is not a retired preacher! He is still preaching, and He is more effective today than He was in His earthly ministry.

Why do I say that? Because while He was here in the flesh, He was limited to one body. He could only be in one place at one time to speak to one group of people. Today He is unlimited because He has many, many bodies — many vessels — and I'm one of them. Right now Jesus is speaking to you through me. While He was here on this earth in the flesh, He declared that He was anointed to preach the Gospel to the poor. Well, I want you to know that He has anointed me to preach this message of prosperity to the Body of Christ.

If you are part of the Body of Christ, then this message is for you, personally. I want to encourage you, to exhort you to pay very close attention to what I will be sharing with you in these pages. If you believe what I'm telling you, then you're going to see some marvelous results from the mighty hand of God, because what I'm telling you is not coming from me, but directly from our Lord Jesus Christ. If you want it to work for you, then receive it just as if Jesus Himself were standing by your side, speaking it directly to you in person.

If you'll open your heart to receive this message, it will revolutionize your whole life. I could share with you testimony after testimony of how it has already affected my own personal life. In fact, when He gave it to me, the Lord said, ''You take these keys of deliverance, these principles that I'm teaching you, and apply them in your own life, and I'll use you as an example to the Body of Christ to show them what will happen to *any* person who will follow them.''

I began to apply these principles to my own life, and I can tell you, it has not been the same since October of 1981! I'm not the same man I was then. This message excites me! It thrills me, because I know it is from God; and it works!

I've received letters from people all over the country who have attended our meetings, who have received what I'm sharing with you now, and their lives have been changed. They've got their priorities in order. They've got their mind on the Provider instead of the provision. That's the key: **God has to be first in your life.**

Jesus said in Matthew 6:33, *Seek ye first the kingdom of God, and his* *righteousness; and **all** these things shall be added unto you.* Jesus is telling us that God wants His people to put Him first so that **they** might prosper. It is my prayer that you will allow the Holy Spirit to speak to you through these pages so He can prosper you for the sake of His Kingdom in these last climactic days before the return of our Lord Jesus Christ.

1

The Purpose of Prosperity

You see, Jesus is on His way. He is coming back very soon. I can almost see Jesus in the spirit realm sitting at the right hand of the Father in heaven. He is resting His arms on the arms of the throne. Every now and then, He leans over to the Father and asks, ''Now, Father?''

''No, not yet,'' replies the Father.

''Now, Father?'' Jesus asks again.

''Not yet.''

''Please, Father, can't I go get them now?''

You see, the Bible tells us that no man knows the hour of Jesus' return except the Father. (Matt. 24:36.) But I want you to know that things are shaping up. Things are happening in the spirit realm. Things are taking place in the physical realm. There are occurrences on this planet right now that cannot be explained by natural man. But *we* can explain them — it's the Holy Spirit on the move! Hallelujah!

The stage is being set right now, and everything is being put in order for the soon appearing of the Lord Jesus Christ. But I want you to know that before He can come, there are whole nations and great multitudes of people who must hear the Gospel. Now I'm not talking about making Baptists, or Methodists, or Presbyterians, or Pentecostals out of people. **I'm talking about making believers out of people!** Children of the Living God!

For generations, we've sent out our missionaries around the world, and I'm sorry to say that in many cases they have done nothing more than take the heathen and make them religious. I've been in many foreign countries and I know what I'm talking about. That's not the plan of God.

God wants an army of people who are members of the Body of Christ — not members of a denomination. He wants an army of believers: people who will dare to stand on His Word without compromise; people who will follow Him and obey Him and serve Him, regardless of what the world thinks, or says, or does; people who won't follow the course of the world, who won't yield to the pressures of the world.

God wants a born-again, Spirit-filled, Bible-carrying, Word-believing, faith-talking, armor-wearing army of soulwinners — and I'm proud to be right in the middle of that crowd! How about you? We are that generation of which the prophets of old would have given anything to be a part.

Someone's always saying something like, ''I wish I had lived when Moses was alive. I wish I had lived when Jesus walked the shores of Galilee.'' Yes, that would have been a thrill. But I want you to know, the best has been reserved for the last generation. I'm glad I wasn't around when Moses lived, or when Elijah was alive, or when Peter walked this earth. I'm glad I wasn't walking side by side with the Apostle Paul. I want you to know, I have the privilege of having Jesus in me right now. Hallelujah!

I am so glad to be a part of the generation that is going to usher in His soon appearing. **We're part of the Church that is going to put Jesus' enemies under His feet!** The Bible says that the last enemy of the Church to be defeated is death. And, thank God, we're the generation that is going to grind death under our heel! Praise God! And do you know why? Because we're so full of life, and so full of God. Wherever God is, there is life — there is no death.

I'm glad I'm part of this generation, part of this army that God is raising up — an army which is standing bold and daring to proclaim to the whole world that Jesus is Lord and that the Word works! I'm glad that we can declare boldly, "If you'll follow me, I'll lead you to victory!" Hallelujah! This is an exciting time in which to live.

Someone might say, "Well, you ought to be around my house. It's not too exciting around there."

Well, then, get in the Word!

"Well, we read our Sunday School quarterly."

I said, *Get in the Word!*

"Well, we've been going to Wednesday night prayer meetings."

I said, ***Get in the Word!*** Don't just sit there and let the Devil beat you. Get in the Word and begin to overcome the world.

I want you to know that God is going to make soulwinners out of every member of the Body of Christ in this last generation. Now, you may not stand before thousands of people. You may not ever be called into an office of ministry. But you're going to fulfill the role of ambassador for Christ like you've never dreamed of fulfilling that role before. **Jesus is going to use you,** praise God, and put you into some special places to reach people who need to be in the Kingdom of God right now.

Some of the people who are resisting the hardest right now had better watch out, because the next thing they know they're going to be preaching the Gospel! Some of the folks who are standing up and declaring that God is dead and that we don't have any business praying or teaching the Bible in our schools had better be on their toes, because before they know it, they're going to be holding prayer meetings! Some of the most influential people of our age are soon going to be witnesses for the Lord Jesus Christ.

In the days ahead, movie and television stars, rock music groups, drug addicts, prostitutes, those into witchcraft and the occult, entertainers, sports figures, and all kinds of celebrities — both famous and infamous — are going to be standing up and preaching the Gospel. God is moving, and Satan cannot stop it!

These are exciting times! Someone has said, ''Well, my brother, don't you know the Devil's running wild? Don't you know that sin is running rampant? Don't you realize that Satan has got all of his messengers out spreading their trash? Can't you see that you can't even turn on your television set anymore without seeing filth? Where have you been, brother? What's the matter with you? Don't you know that the Devil is fighting hard?''

Yes, I know that. I'm fully aware of it. But I also know that where sin abounds, grace does much more abound. (Rom. 5:20.) I want you to know that when the Devil is fighting the hardest, look up, because that's when God is going to come through in a blaze of glory. God is not going to let the Devil get ahead of Him. He never has, and He never will!

This is an exciting time we are living in! I'm glad I'm alive today! And you should be too!

The Bible says that Jesus Christ is coming back for **a glorious Church.** (Eph. 5:27.) This generation is going to be known as ''the glorious Church.'' Notice it didn't say the ''beat-down Church'' or the ''worn-out Church.'' If you listen to what some people are preaching today, you'll get the impression that only a handful of people are ever going to make it to heaven. To hear them tell it, heaven is going to be a great big empty space with just a small handful of folks in it. Well, I don't believe that for a minute.

There is always some poor misguided soul ready to say, "Ah yes, brother, but the Bible says that in the last days even some of the elect will be deceived." That's not so. The Bible doesn't say that some of the elect will be deceived. It says:

*For there shall arise false Christs, and false prophets, and shall shew great signs and wonders; insomuch that, **if it were possible** they shall deceive the very elect.*

Matthew 24:24

. . . *if it were possible.* Jesus was saying here that in the last days false Christs and false prophets would arise to try to deceive people, but that it

21

would be impossible for them to deceive the elect. **If you will get full of God's Word and God's Spirit, there is no demon in hell that can deceive you! You know who you are!**

And who are you? Who are we? We're the generation that is going to usher in the return of the Lord Jesus Christ.

But before that time arrives, there are literally millions around the world who *must* be reached with the Gospel — and that takes money! That's one of the reasons God has called me and given me this message of prosperity to give to the Church. God *wants* us to prosper, for that is the only way His Gospel can ever be given *to every creature.* (Mark 16:15.)

2
Divine Prosperity

And Jesus answered and said, Verily I say unto you, There is no man that hath left house, or brethren, or sisters, or father, or mother, or wife, or children, or lands, for my sake, and the gospel's,

But he shall receive an hundredfold now in this time, houses, and brethren, and sisters, and mothers, and children, and lands, with persecutions; and in the world to come eternal life.

Mark 10:29,30

How is prosperity obtained? Well, we see here that **divine prosperity is the result of a life that is totally dedicated and consecrated to Almighty God.** When we talk about prosperity, we're not talking about taking a principle and selfishly trying to make it work in our personal situation without a dedication and commitment to God. Here Jesus promised a hundredfold return to those who follow Him, but only to those who are first willing to give for His sake and for the sake of the Gospel.

It disturbs me when I see people come into our meetings, hear scriptural principles, then try to go out and make those principles work for them without first developing any kind of relationship with God. Many people who are in financial difficulty try to act on some spiritual principle (such as Jesus' promise of a hundredfold return) without laying any spiritual foundation.

In such teachings as this, Jesus is not giving us some kind of ''get-rich-quick'' scheme. He was teaching a way of life. He was not referring to our giving a portion of what we have, but to our giving our lives. You see, money is a part of our lives. The things that we possess are a part of our very lives.

When we give to God, we can't just give Him one part of our lives, saying, "Now, Lord, I'm going to give You this one part of my life, but You can't have the rest. You can have this one part, but You're not going to be my Lord. I want this to work for me, but I'm not going to do what You want me to. I'm just going to take this one part of my life, this one thing, and invest it in what You're doing, and I want a hundredfold return on it."

No, that's not the way it works. If that's your attitude and intention, you'd be just as well off to keep yours. **Jesus does not want a part of you; He wants all of you.** In fact, I want to tell you something: God will not accept out of His people a divided heart! Either you're for Him, or you're against Him. You either love Him or despise Him. Jesus said:

No man can serve two masters: for either he will hate the one, and love the other; or else he will hold to the one, and despise the other.

Matthew 6:24

You cannot serve two masters. Jesus wants all of you. Before He ever asks for your pocketbook, or your car, or your clothes, or anything you have, what He wants first of all is you! The most important thing you have that God desires and can use is you! If He can get you, then He's got your pocketbook, your bank account, your car, your clothes, and everything else you possess.

But there are so many people who are trying to give just one part of themselves to God and get Him to "pay off on it." They are trying to make a deal with God. "God, You said in Your Word that if I gave I would receive a hundredfold return. I'm giving You this one part of my life. You can't have the rest, just this one part, and now I want to see a hundredfold return on it.'' That's not what Jesus was talking about at all.

Well, then, what was He talking about? To answer that question, let's back up a few verses and see what had happened just before this incident to prompt Jesus to speak to His disciples on the subject of prosperity. We recognize it as the account of the rich young ruler who came to Jesus.

Go and Give

And when he was gone forth into the way, there came one running, and kneeled to him, and asked him, Good Master, what shall I do that I may inherit eternal life?

And Jesus said unto him, Why callest thou me good? there is none good but one, that is, God.

Thou knowest the commandments, Do not commit adultery, Do not kill, Do not steal, Do not bear false witness, Defraud not, Honour thy father and mother.

And he answered and said unto him, Master, all these have I observed from my youth.

Mark 10:17-20

That's the reason he was rich: He kept the commandments! God had promised in the 28th chapter of Deuteronomy:

If thou shalt hearken diligently unto the voice of the Lord thy God, to observe and to do all his commandments which I command thee this day, . . . all these blessings shall come on thee, and overtake thee.

Deuteronomy 28:1,2

God said in Deuteronomy 8:18 that *it is he that giveth thee power to get wealth, that he may establish his covenant.*

So this man told Jesus, ''I've obeyed the commandments of God since my youth.'' That's the reason he was a wealthy man. God had honored the man's obedience to the commandments and had made him wealthy.

Then Jesus beholding him loved him, and said unto him, One thing thou lackest.
Mark 10:21

Now I would like to point out something. Jesus is implying that this man's life was so blessed because he had hearkened to God's commandments, and God had blessed him for it. Jesus said, "But there's only one thing you lack." **One thing.**

That would be nice to hear, wouldn't it? Suppose Jesus appeared to you today and said, "You know, you're doing good. There's only one thing you need to correct." How would that strike you? I don't know many people He could say that to today, do you?

Notice what that one thing was: *Go thy way, sell whatsoever thou hast . . .* (v. 21).

Now many people have read that and have said, "Well, the thing this man lacked was that he had possessions. God doesn't want you to have anything, because we all know that money is the root of all evil.''

Wrong! Nowhere did Jesus imply that God didn't want this man to have things. If God hadn't wanted him to have things, then He shouldn't have blessed him and prospered him for honoring the Word and for obeying the Word. Isn't that so?

Jesus never said that God didn't want him to have things; He *did* want him to have things. What God didn't want was for him to put his trust in those things.

Notice what Jesus told him to do: *Go thy way, sell whatsoever thou hast, and give.*

Go and give. *Go and give.* **Go and give.**

Right there Jesus is pointing out to that man that life does not consist of all

the things we possess. (Luke 12:15.)
Life does not consist of acquiring things
while we're on this planet. Life — the
basic element of life, the very reason
you and I are here on this earth right
now — is not so we can be part of a
census. No! Nor are we here just to take
up space. No! It's not just to fulfill the
scripture where God told Adam to
multiply and fill up the earth with his
kind. No! That's not the reason.

The reason we are here, the very
reason for life being in us right now —
the very reason we've got breath in our
lungs and the ability to think and the
ability to choose, the very reason we are
here as human beings — is to see how
much of ourselves we can give away to
somebody else. Praise God! **Our whole
life consists of giving — not taking,
giving!**

Jesus was not a taker; He was a
giver. Right here He is expressing to

this man the essence of life: *Go and give. Go and give.*

You may be thinking by now, ''Well, I'm tired of preachers always telling us to give.''

In that case, you might as well throw your Bible away, because that's what it's all about. God so loved that He gave. (John 3:16.)

I want to tell you something, sir. When you are in love, you give. Think back to your dating days. You chased that girl around until you married her, didn't you? And all the time you were chasing her, you were giving! Right? Love gives!

And you, Ma'am, when you first got married, you tried your best to please your new husband, didn't you? You went out of your way to do nice things for him, didn't you?

When you're in love, it demands giving. You can't love somebody without giving to them.

I love my wife, so I give. I love my children, so I give. I love people, so I give. I'm a giver. My whole life consists of giving.

Now it wasn't always that way. I used to be a stingy person. My attitude was, ''Man, I worked hard for this, and you're not getting it!''

This was my attitude: ''I don't want anything you've got, and you're not getting anything that's mine!''

But then the Lord Jesus got hold of me and changed my life. All of a sudden, the people I hated the most, I found myself reaching out to. All of a sudden, the people I despised, I found myself loving.

You see, love gives. **Love always gives.** When you truly love someone, you want to give to them. Love isn't selfish. If you love God, then you want to give your whole life to Him. God so loved that He gave. Jesus so loved that

He gave. He gave His life a ransom for many. (Matt. 20:28.)

Here in this passage Jesus is teaching this man the principle of life. He told him, "Go and give." *Go and give.* He was not implying that He didn't want that man to have anything. What He was doing was opening a door to that man's life that was second to none. If you think that fellow was rich before, you ought to have seen what Jesus had in store for him if he had obeyed! *Go and give.* You see, **that's the key to God's prosperity.** Because God so loved, He gave. Because we so love, we give.

You see, if you would fall in love with your pastor, you'd take care of him. "Well, bless God, I just don't agree with everything he preaches. He steps on my toes sometimes. I give only when he preaches what I want to hear."

You ugly thing! If you loved, you'd give.

You may say, "But, brother, I have a hard time loving my pastor."

Well, if you have someone who is hard to love, use your faith. Don't be moved by what you see. Every time you cross his path, grin real big, even if you have to do it by faith. Keep reminding yourself, "I'm not moved by what I see; I'm moved by what I believe. God said to love, and I love that man. I love that man!" Before you know it, God's going to develop His love in your heart, and you'll find that that person is going to become very dear to you.

Did you know that we have the capacity to love even as God loves? Someone has said, "Well, brother, you don't know how ugly these people are. I can't love them." You didn't deserve Jesus. I didn't deserve Jesus. The world didn't deserve Jesus. But *God so loved the world* (it didn't say He loved His own, or that He loved the lovely), *that he gave his only begotten Son . . .* (John 3:16). God so loved that He gave.

So Jesus is teaching this man the principle of life, the principle of living. What is that principle? That life consists of giving. Not taking. Not getting. *Giving.* If your ambition and goal in life is to see how much you can acquire before you die, you've missed the point of life.

Not long ago a man heard me preach this message and he told me about his father. He said that his father had been a very wealthy man. He had been a very close friend to Henry Ford and had accumulated great wealth. In his later years he got born again and turned his life over to the Lord. At that time he was an elderly man and knew that he didn't have much longer to live. So he immediately set out to see how much of what he had accumulated he could give away to those in need. His goal was to give it all away before he went to meet the Lord.

His son told me, ''Brother, I want you to know, he did!''

He gave it all away before he died and went to meet God. When he was saved, his whole idea of living changed. Instead of a life devoted to seeing how much he could get, his life consisted of seeing how much he could give away.

Now I want to tell you something. When that becomes your motivation, when that becomes the driving force on the inside of you — when you love so much that you give — you're not going to have any needs!

Someone has said, "But if I keep giving away, what about me? I won't have anything." No, love doesn't work that way.

When you are activated by the love of God, then so is God. If your life consists of giving, then I want you to know, God will see to it that you don't have any days of poverty, any days of lack, any days of want. If your whole life consists of looking for opportunities to give some of your life away, then, praise God, He's going to be looking for opportunities to give some of His life to you! And, brother, He's got plenty of it to give! "Abundant life," Jesus called it. (John 10:10.)

3

The Danger of Trusting in Riches

Now in telling the rich young ruler to go and give, Jesus was not trying to take anything from him. It was not His intention to deprive this man of any good thing. Why should He? It was God Who had given it all to him to begin with. The Bible tells us: *No good thing will he withhold from them that walk uprightly* (Ps. 84:11). And this man certainly walked uprightly!

No, Jesus was not trying to take from him. He was actually trying to give him some ''good thing.'' He was trying to teach him the basic principle of life — the principle of giving and receiving.

Now notice Mark 10, verses 22,23:

And he was sad at that saying, and went away grieved: for he had great possessions.

And Jesus looked round about, and saith unto his disciples, How hardly shall they that have riches enter into the kingdom of God!

I've heard preachers take that statement and say rich people can't get saved. That's not so. That's not what Jesus said. He said, *How hardly shall they that have riches enter into the kingdom of God.* And He further explains what He means in the next verse:

And the disciples were astonished at his words. But Jesus answereth again, and saith unto them, Children, how hard is it for them (and here's the key) ***that trust in riches*** *to enter into the kingdom of God!*
Mark 10:24

You see, that was the only thing this man lacked. God had blessed him. God had made him wealthy. God had richly poured out His blessings upon his life. But, as a result of it, instead of honoring God with his wealth, he began to put his trust in it. His trust turned from God to his possessions.

Jesus has already taught us that no man can serve two masters. At this point, God is no longer this man's master — his riches are. That fact is evident since he went away sad when Jesus said, ''Go and give.'' **His possessions possessed him.** Instead of his possessing them and making them available to God and others, his possessions possessed him.

Now that's the problem a lot of people are having in our society today. Their possessions possess them. God wants you to have things; He just doesn't want things to have you. Do you understand that? **God does not want things having you.**

Then Jesus went on to say:

It is easier for a camel to go through the eye of a needle, than for a rich man to enter into the kingdom of God.

And they were astonished out of measure, saying among themselves, Who then can be saved?

And Jesus looking upon them saith, With men it is impossible, but not with God: for with God all things are possible.

Then Peter began to say unto him, Lo, we have left all, and have followed thee.

And Jesus answered and said . . . .

Mark 10:25-29

Now listen very carefully to what Jesus is about to say here. Get hold of it. This is the hundredfold principle. But it's not referring to just giving a part of your life to God; Jesus is talking about giving *all* of your life. That is when the hundredfold principle really works, when you give all, not just a part of your pocketbook. Remember, Jesus wants *you*! He wants you before your pocketbook!

The Danger of Trusting in Riches

He said to Peter:

Verily I say unto you, There is no man that hath left house, or brethren, or sisters, or father, or mother, or wife, or children, or lands, for my sake, and the gospel's,

*But he **shall receive** a hundredfold . . . .*
Mark 10:29,30

Now here Jesus is issuing a challenge to His disciples. He is saying to them, "I challenge you to name Me a single man who has given all for My sake or the Gospel's and did not receive a hundredfold in this life."

Jesus was not saying that He wanted His disciples poor. He was saying to them, "Don't *pursue* riches. Don't *trust in* riches. Give Me your all, and I'll give you My all. Put Me first, and I'll put you first. If you'll exalt Me, I'll exalt you. If you promote Me, I'll promote you."

I'll tell you something, you're wasting your time trying to exalt yourself, trying to promote yourself.

When Jesus is doing your exalting, brother, I want you to know it is glorious! Hallelujah!

Persecution For Prospering

But he shall receive an hundredfold now in this time, houses, and brethren, and sisters, and mothers, and children, and lands, with persecutions.

Mark 10:30

Notice, *with persecutions.* Many times we don't want to receive that part, do we? I can guarantee you, if you begin prospering, you'll get persecuted. When the hundredfold principle begins to work in your life, it will be with persecutions. Nobody said much about my prosperity when I had nothing. I didn't have any critics when this principle wasn't working in my life. But you know, when I learned to act on it and benefit from it, brother, you can believe that persecution came with it!

When you start prospering (especially if you're a preacher), let me tell you, there is always going to be someone who won't like it. But, you know, I found out that the persecution can't stop you. The Lord has told me, "Their words are powerless. It's My Word that will get you over."

Once, while I was ministering with T. L. Osborn, he said something to me that I'll never forget. (What a precious man of God Brother Osborn is — a man full of wisdom!) He took me aside and said to me, "Jerry, you are a communicator, and God's going to use you in a great way." Then he said, "I want to warn you about something right now. Don't be moved by the cheers or the jeers."

He said, "There will be some folks who are going to love you, and they'll even worship you, not irreverently, but they'll thank God for you. They'll love you. They'll say, 'Beautiful are your feet.' They'll hold you up and esteem you highly.

"But then there's going to be a group," he said, "who will call your name cursed. They will hate the sound of the message you preach. They will detest the very ground you walk on."

Then he said, "Let me tell you about your critics. [This is what struck me the most.] When people criticize you, receive it as a compliment. That's the only way carnal man has of saying, 'I wish I was like you.' " Think about that.

So then, what's persecution? It's not a drop in the bucket. Some folks are afraid to prosper because of what people will say. Others don't mind a little prosperity for themselves; they just don't think the "man of God" ought to have any!

Let some preacher come to town, riding first class and dressed in the best, and they're ready to tear him to pieces. If he doesn't come on a mule or in a '49 Ford, with his wife dragging behind looking like a Dust-Bowl reject — if he doesn't wear outdated, threadbare suits with shiny seats and knees, old worn-out shoes, and "holely" socks — then to them he's getting rich off the people! If he's not crying and bawling and squalling about how hard it is to live by faith, then he's not spiritual.

The church world has accepted that attitude. Let him come in his own airplane that God gave him, and they think, "He must be hooked up with the Mafia! We don't believe preachers ought to have their own airplanes. Why, bless God, he ought to sell it and give the money to the poor!"

Have you ever noticed how concerned some folks get about the poor when it's somebody else who's supposed to do the giving? About the only connection this kind has with poverty is a "poor mouth."

When you begin to prosper, persecution will come. You will be criticized and opposed. Be prepared for it, but don't let it hinder you. Don't let it stop you. It's not going to stop me. I fully intend to present to this world a first-class Jesus — because that's what He is!

4
The Joy of Giving

When I used to fly on commercial airlines all over the country, I had a great time. I had some great experiences with people I came in contact with on those flights.

You see, I don't particularly look or act like a preacher. I don't go around with a pious look on my face, trying to talk ''spiritual.'' I'm just me, just as natural looking and acting as anybody else. So when I would get on an airplane with all those ''business types,'' dressed nicely, people would often take me for just another ''busy young executive.''

Sooner or later someone would sit down and strike up a casual conversation. You know the kind . . .

"Where are you going?"

"Dallas."

"Me too."

"Oh, really?"

"Nice day, isn't it?"

"Oh, yes. It surely is." (I don't always come out with something "super spiritual." I don't have to let everybody on the airplane know that I'm a preacher.)

Well, one day this fellow sits down by me and we begin talking casually. He asks my name and I tell him. He tells me his name. I ask what kind of work he is in.

"Well, I'm a salesman for a large firm," he replies.

And then he finally gets around to: "And what do you do?"

Now I've been accused of being a lawyer. I've been accused of being in the oil business — and I agree with them on that one; the hidden riches of the earth belong to me. Hallelujah! I've been accused of all kinds of things, but I never tell them that I'm a preacher — just yet!

I say, ''I conduct success seminars all over the United States.''

''Oh, really? Success seminars?''

''Yes.''

''Well, what philosophy do you use?''

''I base all the principles for success on the Word of God.''

You see, he still doesn't know I'm a preacher. It's fun. I mean, in a little while this guy is opening up his whole life to me.

You know, one time I met a man on an airplane like this and by the time we

51

got to where we were going, I was leading him to the Lord. When everybody was getting up to leave, there I was holding this guy's hand and praying with him; so they just stood with their heads bowed. Now that's fun!

But, you know, if I came in there, looking like I had lost my joy, and sat down next to this guy, he wouldn't even want to talk to me.

One time I got on an airplane and a little elderly lady sat down next to me. It was obvious that she was afraid of flying. Oh, she was afraid of that airplane! She was supposed to sit by the window, but she didn't want to be where she could see out, so I moved over and let her sit by the aisle.

She was terrified. She kept saying, "I just know this thing's going to crash. I don't want to fly. I don't like to fly. I told my sister and my daughter that this thing's going to crash and I'm going to die and I'll never see them again. I don't want to do this."

In a moment, I just reached over and held her hand and said, "Ma'am, don't worry about a thing. As long as I'm on board, everything's fine."

She turned and looked at me with a funny expression and said, "What do you mean?"

I said, "Well, I just want you to know that I'm a representative of Jesus Christ and I'm using this airplane to carry the Gospel. I prayed when I got on here and received this machine into my ministry. I want you to know that those people who are flying this airplane work for me today. All these other people are my guests. And no weapon formed against me shall prosper. We won't crash. We're going to have a great time and you're going to enjoy this flight all the way."

She just sat there and held on to me and got rid of all that fear. When we got to our destination, she stood up and said, ''I hope I get to fly with you again.'' Hallelujah! I tell you, it's no burden to work for the Lord; it's a thrill!

Another time I got on an airplane and a lady sat down next to me. In a little while the Spirit of the Lord spoke to me and said, ''You minister to her. She is in financial need.'' I had never seen the woman before in my life. But as I began to study her face, I saw that oppression in her eyes.

I said, ''Ma'am, may I help you?''

She began to weep. She said, ''I'm divorced and I'm trying to raise my children. I've got a funeral to go to. It took every dime I had to get on this airplane. I don't know what I'm going to do.''

I ministered to her for a while. Then in a few minutes I got up and went to the restroom. I got out my checkbook and wrote her a check. When I got back to my seat and sat down, I just leaned over and gave her that check. She began crying, and she said, "But you don't even know me."

"I don't have to know you. You're a child of God, aren't you?"

"Yes, sir, I sure am." Then she said with tears in her eyes, "Before I left home, I prayed and read a scripture. It was the first time I had ever seen that particular scripture. It said, 'My God shall supply all your need according to his riches in glory by Christ Jesus.'" Then she added, "It's so. I've never had anything like this happen to me before!"

I want to tell you, if someone had given me that 707 jet right then, it wouldn't have turned me on anymore than being able to be a blessing to that woman.

Now that's living! That's life. You so love that you give. That's life at its best!

That's what life is all about. It's giving. God so loved that He gave.

Jesus said, "Go and give." That is the essence of living. This is when divine prosperity begins to become a part of your life: when your whole life consists of giving — not trying to get, but to give. So Jesus was telling His disciples, "I challenge you to find Me one man who has lived this way and did not receive a hundredfold in this life, and in the world to come, eternal life."

5

Prosperity Received, Not Pursued

I want you to realize that wealth and riches belong to the children of God. Don't be deceived about this. It may be one of the most powerful things you'll ever learn, and a great help to you in days to come.

Notice that Jesus said, *He **shall** receive an hundredfold.* Remember this: Wealth, riches, and prosperity belong to the children of God; but, **wealth, riches, and prosperity are not to be pursued, they are to be received!**

Did you get that?

Wealth and riches and prosperity are not be sought after. (Jesus said, *Seek* *ye **first** the kingdom of God, and his righteousness.*) They are not to be pursued. They are not to be the inner drive of your existence. Wealth and riches belong to you, but they are not to be pursued. Jesus said that they are received: *. . . and all these things shall be **added unto you*** (Matt. 6:33).

You are to pursue God and Him only. When He is first and foremost in your life — when your whole existence consists of following hard after Him and being His instrument and His vessel — then you are going to receive (not pursue, receive) your hundredfold return.

You see, there are so many people who call themselves ''faith people'' or ''Word people.'' They claim to be pursuing God, but they are actually pursuing riches. They are really pursuing wealth. They are pursuing things, and that's not godly. Things are not to be pursued; they are to be received.

Deceitfulness of Riches

I want to point this out to you from the writings of the Apostle Paul. In 1 Timothy 6:9 we read these words:

But they that will be rich fall into temptation and a snare, and into many foolish and hurtful lusts, which drown men in destruction and perdition.

Now notice: *They that **will be*** (want to be, desire to be, seek to be) *rich fall into temptation and a snare.* Remember, Jesus said in the fourth chapter of Mark that once the Word is sown, *Satan cometh immediately, and taketh away the word that was sown in their hearts* (Mark 4:15). Then Jesus listed five major devices that Satan uses to steal the Word: affliction, persecution, the cares of this world, the lusts of other things, and the deceitfulness of riches.

One of the primary means that Satan uses to get the Word out of the believer's heart is the deceitfulness of riches. Now some people think, ''Well, I won't ever be deceived by riches, because I don't have any.'' If you are pursuing them, you're already deceived.

Riches (that is, the deceitfulness of riches, the pursuit of riches) is an instrument Satan uses to work the Word out of a person's heart, and we can't afford that. We are to protect the Word in our hearts and lives.

When I began to discover that I don't have to try to get prosperous, I began to fully realize who I am and what is mine in Christ Jesus! It suddenly began to dawn on me: **I don't have to try to get wealthy; I am wealthy! I'm a child of the Living God. I'm an heir of God and a joint-heir with Jesus Christ!** I'm not trying to get anything. I've got it! It's already mine! Hallelujah! And as long as I keep my eyes on God, He will manifest it as I need it. He will supply my every need from **His riches** in glory by Christ Jesus. (Phil. 4:19.)

The Love of Money

They that will be rich fall into temptation and a snare, and into many foolish and hurtful lusts, which drown men in destruction and perdition.

*For the **love of money** is the root of all evil.*

1 Timothy 6:9,10

Notice that Paul didn't say money is the root of all evil. He said it was *the love of money* which was the problem.

''Well, then,'' you say, ''I'll never commit that sin because I don't have any money.''

You don't have to have any money to be in love with it. There are probably just as many poor people who love money as there are rich folks who love it. It's not necessary to have money to love it.

That's the reason many people are in jail today, because of their love of money. They lie, cheat, steal, and kill for it. They will do anything, legal or illegal, to get their hands on it. Some of them are in jail because they even tried to manufacture their own! It is this love of money, this lust for money, that is the root of all evil. We, as children of the Living God, cannot pursue riches and wealth and prosperity.

If you are pursuing wealth, it's because you're in love with it. You want it. You desire it. You want it more than anything else. If it means turning away from God to get it, then look out, my friend, you're headed for destruction.

The person whose eyes are on God and whose purpose is to follow Him doesn't have to pursue riches. The riches will pursue him! In Deuteronomy 28:1,2 God tells us:

*If thou shalt hearken diligently unto the voice of the Lord thy God, to observe and to do all his commandments . . . **all these blessings shall come on thee, and overtake thee.***

I'm going to prove to you from God's own Word that He will give prosperity to those who seek after Him and serve Him. There's a difference between taking something and having something given to you. God will prosper you if you will pursue Him and not the prosperity.

Coveting Money

The love of money is the root of all evil: which while some coveted after, they have erred from the faith.

1 Timothy 6:10

"Some folks have coveted money and have erred from the faith," says Paul. You know, there are lot of "faith people" today who are coveting wealth and riches. In so doing, they have "erred from the faith." Did you know that?

You might say, "Why, brother, it sounds to me like you're against faith teaching." That's ridiculous. I'm a faith teacher myself — and a good one too. I'm known around this country as one of the foremost faith teachers of this generation. Why would I want to teach against faith? I live it. It's impossible to please God without it. (Heb. 11:6.)

I'm not teaching against faith. What I'm teaching against is error. What I'm teaching against is deceit. I'm teaching against the things which have caused our priorities to become fouled up so that we have gotten the idea that the whole name of this "faith game" is just get, get, get. It's not — it's give, give, give! That's what faith is all about.

You are not to develop your faith so you can get more things; you are to develop your faith to be an instrument of God!

Following After Righteousness

. . . which while some coveted after, they have erred from the faith, and pierced themselves through with many sorrows.

But thou, O man of God, flee these things (What things? The love of money, the coveting of money); *and follow after righteousness, godliness, faith, love, patience, meekness.*

1 Timothy 6:10,11

These are the things we ought to be following after — the things of God — not money, not riches, not material things.

If you will follow after (pursue) righteousness, godliness, faith, love, patience, meekness, etc., God will see to it that you have all the riches you can possibly use.

That is part of the message Jesus gave to me in His visitation with me. I believe it is going to be a life-changing message for multitudes of people.

We have finally learned some things about *how* to believe God. Now let's get this thing in its proper order and perspective and learn *why* we are to believe God and *what* we are to believe Him for! Let's get our minds off of just accumulating a lot of things and get them onto winning a lot of people! Hallelujah!

If we will follow after God, we'll have all the things we need. He has said so, and I believe it.

Resisting Pride

Now let's look at verse 17:

Charge them that are rich in this world, that they be not highminded . . . .

Now the Lord told me that in the days to come He was going to change the financial status of the Body of Christ, the financial level of those who will believe. So I want to charge you, Christians, be not highminded!

One thing that really grieves my spirit is to see people showing off their prosperity — people putting down other people because they don't have what they've got. I don't like that, and neither does God. That's the reason He said, *Charge them that are rich . . . that they be not highminded.*

You really ought to keep this scripture handy, because your financial status is going to change; and one of the things you will want to guard against when prosperity comes, when riches come, is being highminded.

6
Trusting God, Not Riches

*Charge them that are rich in this world, that they be not highminded, nor **trust in uncertain riches**, but **in the living God** . . . .*

1 Timothy 6:17

It is so easy when your financial status changes to put your trust in the finances rather than the God Who gave them to you. God warns us, "Remember this, it is I Who gave you the power to get wealth. It was not the work of your own hands." (Deut. 8:17,18.)

Riches are uncertain. God is eternal. That's the reason I put my trust in the Almighty God: He changeth not. (Mal. 3:6.)

Inflation has a way of changing riches. Depression has a way of changing riches. Recession has a way of changing riches. But I want you to know that when your trust is in God, He changeth not, regardless of what is happening on earth. It doesn't make any difference if gasoline gets to be $972 a gallon. Our God changeth not! He's got $973, and we're going to go on! Hallelujah!

Don't put your trust in uncertain riches, *but in the living God, who giveth us richly all things to enjoy* (1 Tim. 6:17).

God gives us *richly all things to enjoy.* When? When our trust is in Him and not in riches. That ought to prove to us right there that God's not against our having things. He's the One Who said, ''I'm going to give you richly (not sparingly, but richly) all things (not some things, not just a few things, but all things) to enjoy.'' When? ''When your trust is in Me, when you follow Me and not prosperity or riches or wealth.''

When you put your trust in the Almighty, you will be rewarded richly with all things to enjoy.

Now I'm not suffering. I'm blessed and I've got my trust in the eternal God. People sometimes say, ''Look at him. He gave his life to God, and now he's suffering for Jesus.'' I'm not suffering for Jesus. Jesus suffered for Jerry. The only thing I suffer in this life is persecution, and I can handle that. I'm not going to let it get to me. I don't have to suffer sickness and disease. Jesus suffered that for me. I don't have to suffer the chastisement that was placed upon Him. He suffered that for me. I don't have to suffer poverty or lack or want, because Jesus suffered that for me too. Second Corinthians 8:9 says:

*For ye know the grace of our Lord Jesus Christ, that, though he was rich, yet **for*** *your sakes he became poor, that ye through his poverty might be rich.*

Because of what Christ did for us, God can now freely give us all things to enjoy. Praise God!

Ready To Distribute

Charge them that are rich in this world, that they be not highminded, nor trust in uncertain riches, but in the living God, who giveth us richly all things to enjoy;

That they do good, that they be rich in good works, ready to distribute, willing to communicate;

Laying up in store for themselves a good foundation against the time to come . . . .

1 Timothy 6:17-19

Do you know why God wants you rich? So you can do more. That's why He wants you prosperous. That's why He has reserved the hidden riches of this world for the Body of Christ.

(Is. 45:3.) That's the reason He said the wealth of the sinner is laid up for the just. (Prov. 13:22.) God wants you rich. Why? So you can do even more.

Charge the rich . . . that they be rich in good works. The wealthier you become, the more responsible you are to God. The more prosperous you become, you don't give less to God, you excel in giving. Praise God!

As some people begin to get the financial pressure off of them, as they begin to gain a little prosperity — to get a little money in the bank, get the car paid off, get a little ahead — they start holding out on God rather than increasing their giving. That's the reason their prosperity is going to be temporary.

God said, *Charge the rich . . . that they be rich in good works, ready to distribute.* Isn't that something? Why haven't we seen that before? *Ready to distribute.* God wants us to have everything we've got where it is ready to be distributed. Our home, our car, our bank account, our clothes, everything we possess is supposed to be ready to be distributed at any time. God wants us to possess our possessions, not the other way around. He wants us to hold everything He had given us in readiness, so that when He says, "I have need of that; one of My children has a desperate need for it," we'll be ready to distribute it. Go and give. *Go and give.* **Go and give.**

This is why God wants you out of debt, as He so clearly reveals in Deuteronomy 28:12:

Thou shalt lend unto many . . . and thou shalt not borrow.

God wants us to be in a position where we can lend to many — not a few, but many — and not have to borrow from anyone.

Isn't it going to be exciting to have the shoe on the other foot for a change!

Won't it be great to no longer be the one who is always having to say, "I need," but to hear the other guy say, "I need," and to be able to tell him, "I can give it; I've got it!" Won't that be a welcome change?

Right now your head may be going, *Tilt! Tilt!* You may be saying to yourself, *But I've had to borrow all my life. I can't imagine ever being on the other end. No, that will never work for me.* Hush! Grab your head if you have to and tell it to shut up! Then say, "Thanks, I needed that!"

Change your image. Start seeing yourself the way God sees you. Praise God! There was a time when you couldn't see yourself going to heaven, but you got the Word down in your heart. Now nobody can take it out of you. You know you're going to heaven. If somebody tried to tell you that you are going to hell, you'd say, "Oh, no, I'm not! Bless God, I believe in the Son of the Living God, and I'm heavenbound.''

You changed your perception of your spiritual self, and you can change that self-image of poverty and lack and want. Get the Word down in your heart. Someone may tell you, ''You are going to be on the short end of the stick all your life.'' You tell them, ''No, I'm not! My God meets all my needs. Hallelujah!''

God said, ''Get ready to distribute; be willing to communicate.'' Communicate is just another word for give. *Give.*

God wants His people *rich in good works, ready to distribute, willing to communicate.* As a result they're going to lay up for themselves in store a good foundation against the time to come. God says that the man who gives has a good foundation for anything that comes. You can't destroy the giver. He'll give himself out of every problem.

7

Giving Ourselves

Now let's look for a moment at what Paul wrote to another church about a group of people who were experiencing deep poverty and great trials and tribulation:

Moreover, brethren, we do you to wit of the grace of God bestowed on the churches of Macedonia;

How that in a great trial of affliction the abundance of their joy and their deep poverty abounded unto the riches of their liberality.

For to their power, I bear record, yea, and beyond their power they were willing of themselves;

Praying us with much entreaty that we would receive the gift, and take upon us the fellowship of the ministry to the saints.

*And this they did, not as we hoped, but first **gave their own selves to the Lord**, and unto us by the will of God.*

2 Corinthians 8:1-5

This church was in poverty. They were experiencing many trials and tribulations. Yet they begged and pleaded with the Apostle Paul, "Let us give."

The world would look upon them and say, "How can they give? They're deep in poverty themselves. They don't have anything to give."

They had one thing left, and that was what they were offering to Paul and his ministry. They said, "Paul, we entreat you, let us give you a gift."

Paul said, "What is it?"

"Us! Ourselves! For the ministry of the saints." They didn't have any money, but they had themselves.

Friend, I want you to know, there are a lot of things you can do to help others that money can't buy. There are some folks who need nothing more than for you to put your arm around them and tell them, "You are loved." The freedom it can bring, money can't buy. Many times money is not the answer.

Some people try to use their money as an expression of their love when money is not what's needed. There are some parents who just keep throwing money at their children when what their children really need is some affection — not another toy. That's the reason many people don't like to be around some "rich kids." They've been given everything in the world except what they need — love, affection, and attention. Mama and Daddy were so worried about keeping all their money that they didn't have time to show their children the affection they needed. They just kept buying things for them.

GIVING: The Essence of Living

Sometimes what folks need most is not more money. Sometimes it's just somebody to talk to, someone who will sit down with them and visit with them. There are a lot of things money can't buy.

These people in the Corinthian church didn't have any money. They were in deep poverty, but they begged the Apostle Paul, "Receive our gift, and let us take upon ourselves the fellowship of ministering to the saints." They first gave themselves to the Lord.

They were saying to Paul, "We're going to live by this principle: **The essence of living is giving.** We're going to go and give. All we have to give is ourselves, but we're making ourselves available to the ministry of the saints."

Don't ever tell God that you don't have anything to give. You've got you! You can give yourself, and God will take you. He can use you. **The essence of living is giving.**

The Essence of Living Is Giving

Now let's look at what Paul wrote to the Ephesians:

If so be that ye have heard him, and have been taught by him, as the truth is in Jesus:

That ye put off concerning the former conversation the old man, which is corrupt according to the deceitful lusts;

And be renewed in the spirit of your mind:

And that ye put on the new man, which after God is created in righteousness and true holiness.

Wherefore putting away lying, speak every man truth with his neighbour: for we are members one of another.

Be ye angry, and sin not: let not the sun go down on your wrath:

Neither give place to the devil.

Let him that stole steal no more: but rather let him labour, working with his

hands the thing which is good (Why? So he can make a living? No!), ***that he may have to give to him that needeth.***
Ephesians 4:21-28

Verse 28 is the essence of living: *that he may have to give to him that needeth.*

God said that the reason we ought to be laboring with our hands is so we'll have some seed to sow into someone who needs it. Do you know what God's greatest desire is? That the Body of Christ get to the point that their jobs are not their livelihood, that it is not their jobs which are sustaining their lives, not their paychecks which are meeting their needs. God wants His people to get to the place where Almighty God is doing some superabundant, miraculous things in their lives and causing their needs to be met; and their paychecks are nothing more than seed to sow, to him that needeth. Hallelujah!

There again is the essence of living: giving. God says, ''I want you working with your hands." Why? "So you'll have something to give." Go and give. *Go and give.* Read it aloud: ***Go and give!***

You might say, "Well, dear God, I'm having to hold down three jobs now just to make ends meet!" Change your concept of life. Change your whole idea of what life is all about. Quit thinking that life is *getting*. **Begin to realize that life is giving.** God will begin to work miracles in your life. Praise God!

You're going to find out that this *Jehovah-jireh* — this same God Who supplied manna in the wilderness, this God Who split the Red Sea, this God Who raised Jesus from the dead — is the same God Who careth for thee, the same God Who provideth for thee, the same God Who healeth thee! I don't care if you've never seen a financial miracle in your life, look out! God can still do it, and He can do it for *you*! Praise God! And He *will* do it, if you will do your part.

Servants, be obedient to them that are your masters according to the flesh, with fear and trembling, in singleness of your heart, as unto Christ;

Not with eyeservice, as menpleasers; but as the servants of Christ, doing the will of God from the heart.

Ephesians 6:5,6

Doing the will of God from the heart. What is the will of God? *Go and give.* God so loved that He *gave.* We've already seen that we are to put off the old man and put on the new man which is created after God. Since God so loved that He gave, then we too should love so much that we give.

With good will doing service, as to the Lord, and not to men.

Ephesians 6:7

Every good thing that you're doing, you're doing as unto the Lord — not as unto men.

Knowing that whatsoever good thing any man doeth, the same shall he receive of

the lord, whether he be bond or free.
Ephesians 6:8

Let me change that wording just a little to straighten out your thinking: "Knowing that whatsoever good thing any man doeth, the same shall he receive of the Lord, whether he be *a layman* or *a preacher.*"

Some people have gotten it into their heads that this only works for preachers. They think that because I stand in front of people and preach, people will give to me, but that it won't work for them because they are "just laymen."

No, that's not right. I'm paid a salary, a fixed salary, just like most other people. I, personally, am not a tax-exempt, non-profit organization. No one can receive a tax-deductible receipt for having given to me personally. The money that comes into my meetings doesn't go to me personally; it goes into our ministry. I am paid a salary just like everybody else who works for that ministry. And I can guarantee you, my salary does not meet my needs!

You might ask, "Well, I work in a gas station. How is God going to get it to me?" The same way He's going to get it to me — by faith. *Faith!* **Faith!** Any good thing you do, the Lord is going to see to it that it's done back to you. So start doing some good things!

The next time you're in a store to buy something pretty for yourself, buy something just as nice for someone else at the same time. When you do, you'll find out that somebody is going to start doing that for you. "Any good thing you do, you shall receive the same of the Lord, whether you are bond or free, preacher or layman." This will work for whosoever will do it.

The essence of living is giving.

Now make this confession of faith out loud:

In the name of Jesus, I put my trust in God, not in riches. In Jesus' mighty name, I hereby declare that from henceforth my concept of life shall be, **Go and give.**

The essence of living is giving. From now on, my life consists of giving. I am just like God. God so loved that He gave; therefore, because I love, I give.

I am ready to distribute, willing to communicate. Thank God, I'm a giver, and I have a good foundation for anything that comes.

I am a giver! And my God shall supply all of my needs according to His riches in glory by Christ Jesus!

Praise God!

Jerry Savelle is a noted author, evangelist, and Bible teacher who travels extensively throughout the United States. Jerry teaches the uncompromising Word of God with a power and authority that is exciting, but with a love that delivers the message directly to the heart. His down-to-earth approach and dynamic illustrations clearly present the absolute authority of God's Word.

At the age of twelve as Jerry was watching the healing ministry of Oral Roberts on television, God spoke to his heart and called him into the ministry. Several years later, on February 11, 1969, Jerry made Jesus Christ the Lord of his life.

Since that time, he has been moving in the light of God's calling on his life. Prior to entering his own ministry, Jerry was an associate minister with Kenneth Copeland Evangelistic Association.

The scope of Jerry Savelle Ministries is far reaching. Besides traveling throughout the United States, Canada, and other parts of the world, Jerry is the founder and director of Overcoming Faith Christian School and Overcoming Faith Bible Training Center, both located in Fort Worth, Texas. In addition, Jerry conducts a daily radio program, "Adventures In Faith."

The anointing of God upon Jerry's life is powerful, and people are set free as the Word goes forth unhindered.

For a complete list of tapes and books by Jerry Savelle, write:

Jerry Savelle Ministries
P.O. Box 2228
Fort Worth, TX 76113

GIVING BIRTH TO A MIRACLE

By Jerry Savelle

God is the same God today that He was yesterday: the same God that gave Sarah a son past her age, the same God that created a universe, the same God that birthed Jesus by the Holy Spirit, the same God that entered a fiery furnace and preserved three men from death.

God hasn't changed. He is waiting for us to believe Him. He wants to show Himself strong in our behalf.

In this book Jerry shares how you can enter into the realm of God and give birth to the miraculous in your life.

Another fine book by *Harrison House*

A Right Mental Attitude

The Doorway to a Successful Life

by Jerry Savelle

You will discover how
you can have a daily
positive expectancy.
You will learn that
you can overcome
circumstances in life
and come out of trials
a winner.

A best-selling book
from *Harrison House.*

(CUT ALONG DOTTED LINE)

I WOULD LIKE INFORMATION ABOUT . . . .

☐ PARTNERSHIP . . . in "Adventures in Faith" Television Broadcast

☐ TAPE CATALOG . . . on all of Jerry Savelle's Books and Tapes

☐ MAILING LIST . . . to receive "Adventures in Faith" Newsletter/Magazine and announcements of Special Events.

NAME _____ TELEPHONE _____

ADDRESS _____

CITY _____ STATE _____

ZIP CODE _____